SEND A GIRL!

Jessica M. Rinker   illustrated by Meg Hunt

BLOOMSBURY
CHILDREN'S BOOKS
NEW YORK LONDON OXFORD NEW DELHI SYDNEY

"Brenda Berkman worked where she was hated
so other women could work where they belong."

—Gloria Steinem

BLOOMSBURY CHILDREN'S BOOKS
Bloomsbury Publishing Inc., part of Bloomsbury Publishing Plc
1385 Broadway, New York, NY 10018

BLOOMSBURY, BLOOMSBURY CHILDREN'S BOOKS, and the Diana logo are trademarks of Bloomsbury Publishing Plc

First published in the United States of America in March 2021
by Bloomsbury Children's Books

Bloomsbury books may be purchased for business or promotional use. For information on bulk purchases please contact
Macmillan Corporate and Premium Sales Department at specialmarkets@macmillan.com

Library of Congress Cataloging-in-Publication Data
Names: Rinker, Jessica M., author. | Hunt, Meg, illustrator.
Title: Send a girl! / by Jessica M. Rinker ; illustrated by Meg Hunt.
Description: Hardback. | New York : Bloomsbury Children's Books, 2021. | Includes bibliographical references.
Summary: This dynamic and inspiring picture book biography tells the story of a woman who
broke an important barrier by becoming one of the first female firefighters in New York City.
Identifiers: LCCN 2020028148 (print) | LCCN 2020028149 (e-book)
ISBN 978-1-5476-0174-5 (hardcover) • ISBN 978-1-5476-0175-2 (e-book) | ISBN 978-1-5476-0176-9 (e-PDF)
Subjects: LCSH: Berkman, Brenda—Juvenile literature. | Fire fighters—United States—Biography—Juvenile literature. | Women fire fighters—
United States—Biography—Juvenile literature. | New York (N.Y.). Fire Department—Officials and employees—Juvenile literature.
Classification: LCC TH9118.B47 R56 2021 (print) | LCC TH9118.B47 (e-book) | DDC 363.37092 [B]—dc23
LC record available at https://lccn.loc.gov/2020028148

Art rendered in india ink and black and gray acrylics with digital colors
Typeset in Century Gothic
Book design by Danielle Ceccolini
Printed in China by Leo Paper Products, Heshan, Guangdong
2 4 6 8 10 9 7 5 3 1

All papers used by Bloomsbury Publishing Plc are natural, recyclable products made from wood grown in well-managed forests.
The manufacturing processes conform to the environmental regulations of the country of origin.

To find out more about our authors and books visit www.bloomsbury.com and sign up for our newsletters.

For Brenda, Clare, and every woman who's ever taken the heat —**J. M. R.**

For my mom and all the strong women who made space for me to grow —**M. H.**

Brenda Berkman was a New York City firefighter.
Wherever her officer sent her, Brenda went.

She hauled hoses!
She climbed ladders!
She even broke through walls!
Fighting fires was exciting and gritty,
loud and dirty,
and sometimes dark and dangerous.
Brenda helped save lives and it was the only
job she wanted to do.

For a long time, however, Brenda didn't only fight fires.
She fought discrimination.

When Brenda was growing up in the 1950s, she loved playing sports and being outside. But back then girls weren't allowed to do everything they wanted to do.

Brenda wanted to play baseball.
The coach said, "Don't send a girl to play a boy's game!"

Brenda did NOT like being told she couldn't play sports because she was a girl.
What did being a girl have to do with anything?

So, Brenda and her friends played their own games.
"All-girls football," Brenda said. "We're getting down and dirty!"

As Brenda got older, people's ideas about what boys and girls were allowed to do began to change.

Still, some people had a hard time accepting women in jobs men usually did. Brenda didn't let that stop her. She moved to New York City to attend law school. She hoped to help people.

Brenda liked the idea of being a lawyer, but it turned out to be a lot of sitting still and doing the same thing day after day. She missed being active and outdoors.

Then the New York City Fire Department made a big announcement!
It would finally allow women to take the exam to become firefighters.

Brenda had never thought she'd be allowed to do that.

In the past, every firefighter in the city had to be a man. In fact, they'd only ever been called fire*men*!

Brenda knew firefighting was the job for her.
Firefighters were the first to be called and never knew what to expect. They had to be strong enough to break down doors and smart enough to stay safe.
And most of all, they wanted to help people.

Brenda wanted a job exactly like that.
Firefighting seemed perfect.

But not everyone thought women should become firefighters.

Brenda knew she was courageous, smart, and strong.
She took the written test and passed it.
Now it was time to train for the fitness test.

She ran for miles and worked every muscle. Brenda knew she was ready.

But the fitness test wasn't what Brenda expected.

A firefighter has to be able to carry her own equipment.
She has to be able to break through walls.
She has to quickly solve problems in order to help people.
But this exam didn't test true firefighting abilities.

Every single woman failed.

Brenda believed there were women who were capable of passing the test and becoming trained firefighters. It was clear the fire department wanted to keep women out. Brenda knew she had to stand up for herself and the other women. And it just so happened she had studied law.

Brenda sued the fire department.

And she won.

They had to create a new test that was a good measurement of the ability to be trained as a firefighter.

But some people *still* didn't want
Brenda to succeed.

When she returned to take the new test, the fire department only had men's gear. Everything was too big and got in the way of doing the required tasks.

But that didn't stop her.

She ran and proved she was fast.
She climbed ladders and proved her endurance.
She used a sledgehammer and proved she was strong.
She dragged a dummy low on the ground and proved she could think quickly and rescue people.

Brenda always knew she could do it.
Now everyone else did too.

Brenda, and forty other women, passed that test and became the first professional female firefighters in New York City.

But up ahead was a more difficult test.
One that tried her *inner* strength.

Many people *still* didn't want women in the fire service.
They yelled at Brenda and the other women outside
their firehouses.
They said, "I want to be saved by fireMEN!"

Some of the other firefighters were cruel.
They pulled a lot of pranks.
But these pranks were not funny tricks.
They were mean and dangerous and
sometimes threatened the women's lives.

Fighting fires was hard work, but dealing with this treatment was much harder.

Firefighters need to depend on one another.
Brenda wasn't sure if she could depend on all
her fellow firefighters.
Sometimes it was lonely. Often, she felt invisible.

Brenda wasn't the only woman treated badly. And many were afraid if they spoke up it would only get worse. Or they'd lose their jobs. But Brenda understood the laws and assured them they could stand together. She started a group called United Women Firefighters, so the women would have a safe place to talk about what was happening.

Despite the way she was sometimes treated, Brenda kept doing the job she loved. She had good friends who helped her through difficult times.

Slowly things got better.

As the years went by, every time she helped someone she was reminded how important being a firefighter is. Not only to her, but for the whole city.

Brenda did her job so well she eventually became captain.
Wherever Brenda sent her company, they went.

She hauled hoses!
Climbed ladders!
Broke through walls!
Fighting fires was exciting and gritty,
loud and dirty,
and sometimes dark and dangerous.

But Brenda proved women can be firefighters
even in a big city like New York. She fought
discrimination so girls today can do more than
dream about being a firefighter—they can
actually become one.

A NOTE FROM THE AUTHOR

It's important to tell the stories of the women who have gone before us, women who grew up in a time when people didn't ask what they wanted to be, but instead told them what to do. Fortunately for us, many of these women stood up to discrimination and cruelty in the workplace, paving the way for less struggle in years to come. Because of their bravery, wisdom, innovation, creativity, and ambition, we live in a much more accepting world today. We owe so much to these women—the Modern Trailblazers—and need to hear their stories, to know how they struggled and how they were victorious. Most of all, we need to understand that we, too, can stand up for what we believe in and what we love and can support one another.

I first stumbled upon Brenda's story on the PBS website. It wasn't the firefighting that drew me in, as impressive as that is; it was the courage, persistence, and intelligence with which she fought indescribable discrimination, and often cruelty, for years. I knew I wanted young readers to know her story, which, in some ways, is the story of all the women who have gone before us, challenging and changing the world in various ways. Their resilience is powerful and important.

When I met Brenda, I was all the more convinced her story would resonate with readers of all ages. She fought injustice despite how unpopular it made her. She organized and advocated for other women and continued to serve her community even when the personal cost was staggering. Brenda believes "it is important that young people learn about the struggles and hardships their foremothers experienced and the courage those women displayed in trying to make the world more equitable and just for future generations." Thank you to Brenda, and the other forty women of that first passing class, for blazing the trail to make it a little easier for girls to grow up to become firefighters today.

MORE ABOUT BRENDA BERKMAN

History shows women firefighters as far back as the early 1800s. One of the most famous was Molly Williams, an enslaved woman who was enlisted in New York City's volunteer fire department around 1815. During World War II women stepped up to serve as well. There are probably many women firefighters whose names we'll never know simply because they were not recorded in history books. And even though women were volunteering in various departments around the world by the twentieth century, they were few and far between. When it came to employing women as career paid firefighters in New York City, women were not even allowed to apply. This is where Brenda Berkman enters the story. And she entered it with a bang.

It was officially announced in 1977 that the New York City Fire Department (FDNY) would finally permit women to take an exam to become career firefighters. Firefighting is a trained position, meaning no one goes in knowing all aspects of the job. Applicants are tested—mentally and physically—to see if they will be good candidates for training. But the FDNY did little to prepare for women to apply or be trained. In fact, it was believed they actually made the test more difficult to keep women out.

When no women passed the physical exam, Brenda stepped in. She was the sole plaintiff when she sued the fire department for sex discrimination in 1978, and many people thought she was just trying to stir up trouble. Women weren't asking for standards to be lowered; they were asking for the standards to be job related and therefore a benefit to everyone, including the community. The judge even made her promise under oath that she'd quit her job as a lawyer and become a firefighter if she won the case. That was an easy promise—it's why she was suing them in the first place! She truly wanted the job, so she stood up to the injustice despite the risks. After she won the case, the FDNY had to create a test that was an accurate reflection of the job of firefighting. Brenda and forty other women passed the new job-related exam. By now it was 1982.

Winning the lawsuit and passing the exam wasn't even half the battle. Brenda would say that was the easy part. She also knew that she was pioneering an opportunity for other women. If she and the rest of this first group didn't make it, other women would continue to struggle. Today there are training programs for women preparing for the firefighting exam, and women have been successful firefighters for decades.

The city went through the changes with Brenda. Early in her career she founded United Women Firefighters to help organize and mentor women, knowing they needed to work together and support each other. She became an activist for women firefighters and women in nontraditional jobs all over the world. She was promoted to lieutenant and eventually to captain shortly after the terrorist attacks on the World Trade Center, where she responded on September 11, 2001. She had a successful career of twenty-five years in the fire department serving her community in a secure and salaried job previously reserved for men. It was a job she'd fought for, excelled in, and truly loved.

But her story doesn't end there.

When she retired from the fire service in 2006, she was ready to do so. She wondered what she would do next. How would she go from a physically and mentally demanding career to a quiet retirement? The transition would prove to be her next challenge. She began volunteering at the 9/11 Tribute Museum, giving tours and talks on her experiences. She continues as a public speaker, advocate, and activist for women's equality. She's also working with an all-volunteer group, Monumental Women, to put up the first statue of real women in New York City's Central Park.

Brenda also began an entirely new endeavor, one that seems quite a bit different from the gritty, brave job of being a firefighter, and requires courage of a different kind. Instead of dealing with danger and destruction, Brenda now creates. One of her talents is making beautiful lithographs of New York cityscapes, including a series called "Thirty-Six Views of One World Trade Center" that documents the rebuilding of the World Trade Center. Perhaps in an effort to heal her own heart and the heart of the city after the horrific attacks of September 11, 2001, Brenda has found a way to send herself, gracefully, into the next part of her life.

BIBLIOGRAPHY

BRIC TV, producer. *Meet Captain Berkman, One of NYC's First Women Firefighters*. Brooklyn, NY: BRIC TV, September 27, 2017. https://www.youtube.com/watch?v=grC7BTDh7mE.

Career 2.0. (blog). "Brenda Berkman: From Pioneering Firefighter to Printmaker." July 17, 2014. https://careertwodot0.wordpress.com/2014/07/17/brenda-berkman-from-pioneering-firefighter-to-printmaker/.

Fried, Joseph P. "Women Win Ruling on Fire Dept. Test." *New York Times*, March 6, 1982.

May, Clifford D. "Court Refuses Suit by Women Over Fire Test." *New York Times*, October 6, 1987.

Otis, Ginger Adams. "New York's First Black Firefighters," *The History Reader*. May 29, 2015. https://www.thehistoryreader.com/historical-figures/black-firefighters.

Reynolds, Josephine. *The Extraordinary Story of Britain's First Female Firefighter*. London: Michael O'Mara Books, 2017.

Rinker, Jessica M., personal interview with Brenda Berkman, August 2017.

Roy, Bann, dir. *Taking the Heat: The First Female Firefighters of New York City*. Independent Lens, 2006.

Stabiner, Karen. "The Storm Over Women Firefighters." *New York Times*, September 26, 1982.

WEBSITES FOR FURTHER READING

African American Firefighter Museum
www.aaffmuseum.org/woman-of-fire/

Brenda Berkman
www.brendaberkmanartworks.com

Labor Arts
www.laborarts.org/exhibits/womenfirefighters/1982-87.cfm

Makers: The Largest Video Collection of Women's Stories
www.makers.com

Sisters in the Brotherhoods
www.talkinghistory.org/sisters/berkman.html

United Women Firefighters
www.unitedwomenfirefighters.org

Women You Should Know
womenyoushouldknow.net